Promise

&

Praise

Advent Word Reflections

Richelle Thompson • Hugo Olaiz

Miriam McKenney • Scott Gunn

With Michael B. Curry and Lisa Kimball

Scripture quotations are from the New Revised Standard Version of the Bible, copyright © 1989 National Council of the Churches of Christ in the United States of America. Used by permission. All rights reserved. Psalm passages are from the Psalter in The Book of Common Prayer.

ISBN: 978-088028-501-8
Printed in USA

Forward
Movement

www.forwardmovement.org

Promise

&

Praise

Advent Word Reflections

Richelle Thompson • Hugo Olaiz

Miriam McKenney • Scott Gunn

With Michael B. Curry and Lisa Kimball

FORWARD MOVEMENT
Cincinnati, Ohio

Introduction

Advent calendars play a prominent role in our home. Over the years, we've marched through the season by opening flaps on a bucolic scene of a manger under a starry sky. Hidden behind windows in various calendars, chocolate treats and Lego pieces and even bracelet charms have helped us count the days to Christ's birth.

As a writer and a lover of words, I can think of no better way to mark time than with AdventWord. Reflecting on one word each day of the season of Advent offers a special intentionality, a way to countdown to Christmas, focused on God's promise in a posture of praise.

The AdventWord initiative began in 2012 with the brothers of Saint John the Evangelist as a way to move through the season one day and one word at a time. The goal was a practice that is both particularly individual, with each person contemplating the day's word, and purposefully communal, with people sharing pictures and stories on social media.

As AdventWord grew, Virginia Theological Seminary began shepherding the initiative and expanding its reach through new social media channels. In 2021, the seminary graciously turned over stewardship of AdventWord to Forward Movement. We are delighted to build upon their good work and grateful for their continued participation.

Under the leadership of longtime project manager Sarah Stonesifer Boylan, AdventWord continues as an online, dynamic calendar, filled with brief daily reflections in English, Spanish, French, and American Sign Language and visual images, augmented by contributions from around the world. The words for each day of this journey were drawn from the Sunday scripture readings and prayerfully selected by a diverse team of church leaders. The longer meditations in this book provide an opportunity to spend more time with each word. The Spanish and French translations are included with each meditation.

We hope you'll participate however you feel called—this year and in years to come. *Promise & Praise* is designed with enough daily readings for even the longest season of Advent. If you're reading in a year when Christmas comes earlier in the fourth week of Advent, simply skip ahead to the Christmas Eve and Christmas Day readings (and consider the extra meditations a bonus!)

In a world that likes to rush, it's easy to jump ahead in the story, to the words we know by heart of a babe born in a manger. But AdventWord calls us to slow down, to be tender in our expectation, to offer praise and glad tidings, so we may fully prepare for the fulfillment of God's promise.

Richelle Thompson
Managing Editor
Forward Movement

Ways to Connect with AdventWord

AdventWord.org

facebook.com/AdventWordOrg

Twitter & Instagram: @AdventWord

The AdventWord podcast is available on all streaming platforms, including Apple Podcasts, Spotify, Stitcher, and anywhere else you listen to podcasts.

Make sure to tag #AdventWord or our official accounts!

Readings for the First Sunday of Advent

Psalm 25:1-9
Jeremiah 33:14-16
1 Thessalonians 3:9-13
Luke 21:25-36

PROMISE
PROMESA   PROMESSE

Let us hold fast to the confession of our hope without wavering,
for the one who has promised is faithful.
—HEBREWS 10:23

Advent is, of course, a season of hopeful expectation, pressing on toward the promise. It could very well be said that all of life is about hopeful expectation, pressing on toward the promise despite the long, hard journey we face. Indeed, throughout the biblical narrative and the church's history, we encounter faithful people hanging on to hope, sometimes by a slender thread, clinging to a promise far removed from their harsh reality.

Some caught a glimpse of something glorious as they struggled on. As Martin Luther King Jr. proclaimed before he was slain, "I have seen the promised land." Like Moses before him and far too many others through the ages, Dr. King did not witness the full realization of that promise. But he caught a glimpse, and in his life, he shared a dream of justice and equality and opportunity for God's children…for ALL God's children. He held fast to hope, refusing to waver, and he urged others to do the same.

At times, it is difficult to still see the promise through the fog that envelops us, the storm that bears down on us. Life can be so very hard and the forces of darkness so overpowering that we might understandably be tempted to give up, to let go of the hope, to let go of the dream. Yet, as the psalmist notes, even in "the valley of the shadow of death," we are not alone; the Shepherd is with us. We make our song, "O Come, O Come, Emmanuel," precisely because we dare to believe in Emmanuel, God with us. And if God is indeed with us, God is with ALL of us. The promise endures. The hope—the dream—remains sure…despite the fog and storm, despite the darkness.

As a prophet and bridge-builder in South Africa both during the wicked time of apartheid and in the years since, Archbishop Desmond Tutu has said, "Your ordinary acts of love and hope point to the extraordinary promise that every human life is of inestimable value." Through our small and seemingly insignificant acts of kindness and care each day, we commit ourselves once more to the promise. By speaking up and standing up for those who are being silenced and pressed down, we proclaim that we refuse to waver in our hope of the promise.

The promise of a world that is Beloved Community is real and true, and we are its ambassadors, heralds of the Way of Love, for God's sake and for the sake of ALL God's children.

—Michael B. Curry

Lord, you now have set your servant free to go in peace as you have promised; for these eyes of mine have seen the Savior, whom you have prepared for all the world to see: a Light to enlighten the nations, and the glory of your people Israel.

—The Book of Common Prayer, p. 140

Strength
Fortaleza   Force

Too often, strength is confused with might.

But time and again, scripture tells us strength is not the ability to outmuscle someone or something. It is not an Instagram snap of a barbell jerk, hoisting hundreds of pounds to our chest and shoulders. It is not clawing our way to the top, intent on emerging as the lone victor.

Rather, strength is the fortitude of a mother to gather her sons and the last bit of cash and start over in a new town and a strange state so they might be protected from the calamities of a derelict father.

It is the woman born with no arms and legs who paints and cooks and inspires others with words of hope and expectation.

Strength is seeking out "good trouble," pushing back against injustice, on bridges and streets, in classrooms and courthouses. And strength is a community refusing to be bowed by a virus, with neighbors checking in on one another, drawing notes of encouragement in chalk on sidewalks, gathering virtually and at the end of driveways to nurture bonds of affection.

David fells Goliath with the strength of faith, a slingshot, and a stone, and Mary's strength lies in her unequivocal yes to an unimaginable request. We have the ultimate example of strength in Jesus, who bloody and dying, still thinks of others, asking God to forgive us for we know not what we do.

And yet, we still conflate strength with force and elevate the strong-armed. We forget that true strength comes in making peace with our weaknesses, in offering our raw and vulnerable selves in service of others. Strength is principle and compassion, selflessness and sacrifice.

Dear Lord, let me be strong like that. Help me set my heart on the pilgrim's way, happy to have my strength in you.

—*Richelle Thompson*

O God, the strength of all who put their trust in you: Mercifully accept our prayers; and because in our weakness we can do nothing good without you, give us the help of your grace, that in keeping your commandments we may please you both in will and deed; through Jesus Christ our Lord, who lives and reigns with and the Holy Spirit, one God, for ever and ever. *Amen*.

—The Book of Common Prayer, p. 216

SOUL
ALMA   ÂME

To you, O LORD, I lift up my soul; my God, I put my trust in you.
—PSALM 25:1A

The opening verses of Psalm 25 provide a lovely invitation to reorient our lives away from self-centered living and toward the true and living God. Our fancy church word for this is repentance. Repentance means turning in a new direction, starting with a clean slate, changing our destination in life. Repentance is the very essence of Advent.

This short season encourages us to prepare to meet Jesus. Perhaps we are preparing to meet him when he comes in glory. Or maybe we will meet him first when we die. Of course, Advent also points us toward our worship of Jesus at Christmastime. Wherever and whenever we meet Jesus, we need to be ready. But how do we do that?

Psalm 25 gives us some help. To lift up our souls to God is to dedicate our very lives to God. To trust God means that we depend on God's grace, not on human power or earthly wealth. But what does that look like, exactly?

Much of the psalm reminds us that we need to learn God's laws. This might seem foreign or even unpleasant to us. You mean we have to follow laws?!

The thing is: God's laws lead us to true freedom. They help us live as God hopes we might live. God's laws pull us away from selfish impulses and toward the sacrificial love that Jesus showed us.

God tells us to love our enemies. We are commanded to welcome strangers. We should give generously of what we have to those who have less than us, and we should give generously so that God's work can be carried out in the world. God expects us to tell the truth. God's law favors mercy.

You get the idea. In the assigned scriptures for Advent, we encounter stirring prophets calling us to change. We meet those who prepared the way for Jesus. We see that the world wasn't right before Jesus lived among us, and it still isn't right as we wait for Jesus to come in glory.

Advent is my favorite season, but I need to take care never to make the mistake of thinking Advent is a time for sentiment and nostalgia. The liturgical season of Advent is a bit like the voice crying out in the wildness, inviting the church to prepare the way of the Lord.

May we all lift up our souls to God. May we all be ready to meet Jesus, whether in this life or the life to come.

—Scott Gunn

Almighty God, you know that we have no power in ourselves to help ourselves: Keep us both outwardly in our bodies and inwardly in our souls, that we may be defended from all adversities which may happen to the body, and from all evil thoughts which may assault and hurt the soul; through Jesus Christ our Lord, who lives and reigns with you and the Holy Spirit, one God, for ever and ever. *Amen.*

—The Book of Common Prayer, p. 218

PATH
SENDERO   CHEMIN

Around six years ago, I ventured onto a trail in the woods of
one of our county parks called the Kingfisher Trail. A sign at
the trailhead included a map of the route and indicated it was
a little over a mile long. It was a lollypop trail, where you walk
in straight and then go left or right in a circle. The path turns
sharply to go uphill in one direction or downhill in the other.

On this day, I chose to go uphill first, while I had more
energy. Once I completed the circle and turned toward the
path out, I decided I'd made the right choice. I visited the
trail often, usually turning right to go uphill. One day, I
decided to go the other direction, downhill toward a creek
that ran through the park. The seasons had changed from fall
to winter, and even though there was snow and ice, I thought
I'd be fine. I knew this trail. I had a map, not that I needed it.

That day I learned that no matter how much I knew about that trail, I didn't know everything. I didn't consider the parts of the path that would ice over and freeze near the creek. I didn't realize the stone steps I usually go down would be too dangerous, forcing me to turn around and go back across the icy path. Nothing went the way I expected, even though I had prepared with proper gear and clothing. I thought I had everything I needed, and in the end, I did. I had God with me on that path. I let the Spirit guide my decisions to keep me from falling.

In Psalm 25, the psalmist implores God: *Show me your ways. Teach me your paths. I trust you, God.* My trail adventures remind me that we must keep asking God to show us, to teach us God's paths. When we think we've learned enough, it's time to ask again. Things change in the woods just like they change in our walks of faith. When we get comfortable with the path we are on, we should call on God to teach us something new about our course—or perhaps even a new way. According to the psalmist, "all the paths of the LORD are love and faithfulness to those who keep his covenant and his testimonies" (Psalm 25:9).

As we keep our covenant of Advent waiting, let us follow God's path of love and faithfulness to the birth of God's love and faithfulness to God's people—a baby born in Bethlehem. God, guide us on this Advent path of love.

—*Miriam McKenney*

Grant us patience, O Lord, to follow the road you have taken. Let our confidence not rest in our own understanding but in your guiding hand; let our desires not be for our own comfort, but for the joy of your kingdom; for your cross is our hope and our joy now and unto the day of eternity. *Amen.*

—Saint Augustine's Prayer Book, p. 235

Justice
Justicia   Justice

In the year 1999, when many feared that the Y2K computer bug would cause major disruptions in our lives (and some imagined an Apocalypse of sorts), my friend Michael sent me a copy of survival tips published in the satirical paper *The Onion*. The list concluded: "If disaster strikes, it's God's wrath–quote the Old Testament. But if nothing happens, God is merciful— quote the New Testament." The statement captures the striking contrast we sometimes see between the way God is presented in the Old Testament (harsh and vengeful) and the New Testament (loving and compassionate). The problem, of course, is that when we actually read the Bible, we find all kinds of nuances. God's concept of justice, it turns out, is a lot more complex than we think.

Many of Jesus's teachings focus on the connection between God's justice and our human attitudes toward justice—particularly in the way we see and treat others. In the Parable of the Workers in the Vineyard (Matthew 20:1-16), a landowner hires laborers for his vineyard, some early in the morning, some a few hours later, and some at five o'clock. At the end of the day, no matter how many hours they worked, they all receive the same pay. Those who worked all day complain—not necessarily because the Lord paid the latecomers in full, but because they thought that they, having come so early, deserved more. This parable, along with the Prodigal Son and the Jealous Brother (Luke 15:11-32), dramatizes the dangers of feeling entitled or believing we deserve more and better than others.

When I was younger, I tended to see God's justice as the supernatural intervention of a God who decided when to punish and reward. Today my views are more nuanced. I believe that many sins carry their own punishment. Above all, I believe that we can have an active role in bringing about God's justice. After witnessing God's spectacular judgment over the whole world, John of Patmos sees "a river of the water of life, bright as crystal, flowing from the throne of God" and a tree of life that produces fruits and leaves "for the healing of the nations" (Revelation 22:1-2). At this time, when human life is threatened not just by hatred and wars but also by polluted waters and the destruction of natural habitats, I find it easy to equate pure waters and fruitful tress with celestial bliss. Could we begin to see our solar panels, community gardens, and environmental laws as ways to help bring to pass John's vision for a just world?

—*Hugo Olaiz*

Almighty God, who created us in your own image: Grant us grace fearlessly to contend against evil and to make no peace with oppression; and, that we may reverently use our freedom, help us to employ it in the maintenance of justice in our communities and among the nations, to the glory of your holy Name, through Jesus Christ our Lord, who lives and reigns with you and the Holy Spirit, one God, now and for ever. *Amen.*

—The Book of Common Prayer, p. 260

FULFILL
CUMPLIR   ACCOMPLIR

The scholars who created the King James Bible used a 1568 English translation known as the Bishops' Bible. In Luke 1:57, the verse in which we are told that Elizabeth gave birth to John the Baptist, they read: "Elizabeth's time came that she should be delivered." The translators corrected the text and wrote: "Elizabeth's time was fulfilled that she should be delivered." But still unconvinced, they crossed it out and wrote: "Elizabeth's full time came that she should be delivered." In the BBC documentary *When God Spoke English*, author Adam Nicolson and Bible scholar Gordon Campbell celebrate this correction. Not only is it more faithful to the original (the Greek verb *plétho* means "to furnish" or "to fill"), but also it denotes a sort of triple full-fill-ment: the fulfillment of the prophecy the angel gave Zechariah (Luke 1:13), the fulfillment of the term of Elizabeth's pregnancy, and (we would like to think) of Elizabeth's full belly!

The fulfillment of prophecies is typically a tricky business because it happens in God's due time and often in ways we never imagine. For example, the gospels suggest that at a time when Israel was expecting a Messiah who would wage wars and restore Israel, Jesus came to tell them to turn the other cheek and announced, "My kingdom is not from this world" (John 18:36). The dissonance between the fulfillment we expect and the one God provides creates tensions. In fact, I wonder if many of our personal frustrations, estranged relationships, and even church conflicts happen because we fail to understand or accept this dissonance. In religious contexts, this dissonance can be particularly hard because we have been trained to believe that God hears our prayers and blesses our good intentions.

As a general rule, I tend to think that God moves in mysterious ways and that I "see through a mirror, dimly" (1 Corinthians 13:12). Yet, there have been a few times in my life when I have clearly sensed the fulfillment of God's purposes. Perhaps what makes Elizabeth's story so iconic is that the "fullness" of her pregnancy (her full-fill-ment) was aligned with the fulfillment of God's promises to a whole nation: the angel had told Zechariah that their son, John the Baptist, would turn "many of the people of Israel to the Lord their God" (Luke 1:16).

Could this be one of the keys to personal fulfillment—when we find that our personal fulfillment is aligned with the fulfillment of our loved ones, our neighbors, and those with whom we work and worship?

—*Hugo Olaiz*

Dear God, who lives and reigns in perfect unity with the Son and the Holy Spirit: So align our hearts and minds with your divine purposes, that we may be instruments of peace and reconciliation, fulfilling your designs and helping the whole world become one under your gracious oversight. *Amen.*

HEART
CORAZÓN   CŒUR

And now, O Lord, I bend the knee of my heart, and make my appeal, sure of your gracious goodness.
—PRAYER OF MANASSEH 11
THE BOOK OF COMMON PRAYER, P.213

When I pray Morning Prayer, I always love this line as it comes up in the *Kyrie Pantokrator* (Canticle 14). Bending the knee of my heart is such an evocative image.

The heart is vital to our bodies. Beating billions of times in an average human lifetime, it only takes a little glitch of the heart to change everything. So naturally, we work to take care of our hearts. We eat foods that are good for our hearts. We exercise to keep our hearts in tip-top shape.

I have a leaking valve in my heart. It's a fairly common condition that I control with medication for now. Someday,

I may need surgery. Because of this condition, I visit a cardiologist once or twice a year to check up on my heart. Each time I am amazed when it's time to get an echocardiogram, and I get to see my own heart pumping away. Beat, beat, beat, beat.

In the Bible, hearts are understood not just as organs that keep us alive but as vital centers in our moral life. People who need to repent have their hearts of stone removed to be replaced with a heart of flesh (Ezekiel 36:26). People who are unable to repent have hardened hearts (Hebrews 3:8). And those who need to repent must be humbled, bending the knees of our hearts.

Advent invites us to be ready for Jesus when he comes in glory. For that reason, 1 Thessalonians offers some advice. "And may he so strengthen your hearts in holiness that you may be blameless before our God and Father at the coming of our Lord Jesus with all his saints" (1 Thessalonians 3:13).

I don't know about you, but I know my heart isn't strong in the way that keeps me blameless! Wouldn't it be nice if there were a way to get a glimpse of the beating of our moral hearts the way the echocardiogram gives us a glimpse of our pumping hearts?

The church does, in fact, offer such a check-up. The rite of reconciliation, sometimes called confession, invites us to take a thorough moral inventory of our lives. There are self-examination prompts in several places, including the *Saint Augustine's Prayer Book* from Forward Movement. When we make our confession, we can fearlessly catalog our moral failings and shortcomings because we know that the priest will never reveal what we have said. During the confession, the priest may offer counsel or support in our inevitable need to repent.

Keeping care of our moral hearts is every bit as important as caring for our pumping hearts. Both are essential to living, one for our eternal lives and one for our earthly lives.

How is your heart?

—*Scott Gunn*

Almighty God, you have poured upon us the new light of your incarnate Word: Grant that this light, enkindled in our hearts, may shine forth in our lives; through Jesus Christ our Lord, who lives and reigns with you, in the unity of the Holy Spirit, one God, now and for ever. *Amen*.

—The Book of Common Prayer, p. 213

Readings for the Second Sunday of Advent

Canticle 4 or 16
Baruch 5:1-9 or Malachi 3:1-4
Philippians 1:3-11
Luke 3:1-6

PRAISE
ALABANZA   LOUANGE

My friend, Mary W. Cox, began a practice several years ago
of walking each day. She soon married the practice with
a discipline of writing. Inspired by her walks or the day's
events, she writes remarkable haikus, somehow bending
the very specific structure of this Japanese form of poetry
into a provocative snapshot—all in seventeen syllables. She
graciously shares these poetic gifts on her social media and
here, in this meditation.

These poems are like modern-day psalms, responding and
reflecting on the breadth of life, the grace and glory, the
agony and loss. They are a tangible witness to the praise
we are called to offer God: for the beauty of creation, the
thoughtfulness of a shade tree, the splendor of the ocean,
the whisper of butterfly wings. We should praise God for
songs and friends, long lunches and new books, spouses and
children and parents and siblings, and all the many gifts given
freely to us.

Often Mary delights in the wonders of creation. With a keen eye and a curious spirit, she zooms in on the curve of a flower, the work of a bee, the leaves of the trees:

> Bent down, daffodil
> trumpets through pine straw, "Hear me,
> cold earth: Spring will come."

> If there's a clean slate,
> rain washed it—gutters filling
> with sky, trees, lost leaves.

At other times, Mary succumbs to whimsy, inspired by yard signs and street litter and even the purchase of new shoes:

> Breaking in new shoes—
> or maybe just retraining
> some old worn-out feet.

And then there are the difficult days, when it would be easy to turn from praising God. When we heave and holler, lash out and crumple in, and when we mourn:

> Every day this year—
> lost, some ordinary thing
> we took for granted.

Mary's words join the psalms in reminding us to praise God not only in the feast but also in the famine, for God is always with us. "The Lord upholds all those who fall…[and] near to those who call upon him" (Psalm 145:15,19). And that is worthy of praise indeed.

—Richelle Thompson

Light born in darkness,
song in silence—empty hearts
now cradle of Love.

Connected by need—
the world's, our own—Love's hand, scarred,
reaching out, joins us.

Amen.

EVERLASTING
ETERNO   ÉTERNEL

Everlasting God. Everlasting Love. Everlasting traffic. These thoughts entered my mind as I read the list of Advent words, deciding which to select to write my meditations. As my eyes rested on everlasting, my mind dove into the word. Since I think of everlasting as a modifier, I was drawn to this word used here as a noun, and even more interestingly, a place.

Part of our process for writing these meditations is choosing the words from the Advent lectionary about which we will each write. We write the meditations months after we select the words from the lectionary readings. When I picked path and everlasting, I didn't realize that they were both from Psalm 25. Those two words simply called me.

Words are like that, which is why choosing a favorite translation of the Bible is essential. I encourage you to choose one that you enjoy reading, one that challenges you, one that has words that call you to them, again and again, to read, mark, and inwardly digest. I decided that God has something to tell me, and us, with Psalm 25.

Remember, O Lord, your compassion and love, for they are from everlasting. Most translations use "of old" instead of "everlasting" to capture the origin of God's compassion and love. As I meditated on the word everlasting, verses from John 1:1-18 came to my mind, as recounted in the Common English Bible. "In the beginning was the Word and the Word was with God and the Word was God. The Word was with God in the beginning. Everything came into being through the Word, and without the Word nothing came into being. What came into being through the Word was life, and the life was the light for all people…The Word became flesh and made his home among us. We have seen his glory, glory like that of a father's only son, full of grace and truth."

Everlasting comes closer to God in that God's compassion and love are not old. They are old and new, now and what was and what will be. In my early ruminations about the word everlasting, I thought of ways we use it to mean a long time. Winter does not last forever. Unlike in the book *Willy Wonka and the Chocolate Factory*, when you eat an everlasting gobstopper, it won't last forever. Only God's love and compassion lasts forever and comes from forever. That's good news!

God's mercy and love know no beginning or end. God loved us before we were born and offers us unlimited grace. We do well to consider how much God loves us and has compassion on us to set us on this path of waiting for the manifestation of God's eternal love for us, God's Son, Jesus.

—*Miriam McKenney*

Direct us, O Lord, in all our doings with your most gracious favor, and further us with your continual help; that in all our works begun, continued, and ended in you, we may glorify your holy Name, and finally, by your mercy, obtain everlasting life; through Jesus Christ our Lord. *Amen.*

—The Book of Common Prayer, p. 832

OFFERING
OFRENDA   OFFRANDE

It had been a big weekend. There was the press conference
with Nobel Peace Prize winner Archbishop Desmond
Tutu, in town to celebrate the retirement of his good friend,
Bishop Herbert Thompson. Hundreds of people from across
Southern Ohio came to honor their beloved bishop, and
special events filled the calendar. For the diocesan staff, the
weekend was the culmination of months of planning. It was
exhausting and exhilarating and bittersweet: we were grateful
that we had the chance to send into retirement our good
bishop with glad tidings and already beginning to mourn
his absence.

I ducked into the last pew at the cathedral just as worship
started. In this grand service, the cathedral pulled out all
the stops. Long streamers waved high above the pews in
procession. Voices of the choir soared, and clergy of all sorts
dressed in their finest walked the aisle and toward the altar.

I should have been completely enchanted by the service, but I was mostly glad for a semi-comfortable place to sit, some time off my feet, and a break from responsibilities. I didn't notice the man slide into the pew next to me until I caught a whiff.

In a cathedral full of the well-heeled, this man was the exception. He wore an old Army jacket and low-slung pants, boots with one of the soles flapping, and what seemed to be a dirty kerchief wrapped around his neck. Rheumy eyes glanced my way, and a head bob nodded acknowledgment. I scooted over.

The aerobics of an Episcopal service isn't a friend to the weary, but nevertheless, we stood, sat, and kneeled with the rest of the congregation. The sermon went on long enough that I had to shake myself awake; I was jealous of the deep breathing and low snores of my pew companion. When it came time for the peace, he roused and turned to shake my hand. I didn't expect the softness of his skin, and his warmth lingered.

The ushers gathered at the back with offering plates, and I fished out my wallet. A twenty and two ones. I did some quick mental calculations. I might need the twenty for parking or, and I'm being honest here, a drink at the hotel bar at the end of the night. I grimaced, knowing that two dollars seemed chintzy, but I was being practical, thinking ahead.

I placed the dollar bills in the plate and then passed it to my pew mate. He dug into his pocket and pulled out a handful of change.

He did not stop to count or pull out the quarters or check to make sure he had some money left for later. He dropped all of it into the plate. Like the widow's mite, his offering was complete. Without pause. Without guile.

His offering was sacrificial. Mine was obligation. He gave all he had. I gave what I was willing to spare.

Who was rich and who was poor? That day, the answer was clear, and I bowed my head to pray for forgiveness.

—*Richelle Thompson*

Let us with gladness present the offerings and oblations of our life and labor to the Lord.

—The Book of Common Prayer, p. 377

MESSENGER
MENSAJERO   MESSAGER

*See, I am sending my messenger to prepare the way before me,
and the Lord whom you seek will suddenly come to his temple.
The messenger of the covenant in whom you delight—indeed, he
is coming, says the Lord of hosts.*

—MALACHI 3:1

Every Sunday when we gather for Holy Eucharist, we hear
a brief summary of our salvation history. In Prayer B, it goes
like this:

> We give thanks to you, O God, for the goodness and love
> which you have made known to us in creation; in the calling
> of Israel to be your people; in your Word spoken through the
> prophets; and above all in the Word made flesh, Jesus, your Son.

—The Book of Common Prayer, p. 368

It's a good reminder to us that God our Father has desired our salvation from before time until this very moment. God made the world good. God sent prophets and messengers into the world to call us to repentance. Finally, God sent his own Son into our world to be for us "the exact imprint of God's very being" (Hebrews 1:3). Everything we need to know about God we can see in the life, teaching, suffering, death, and resurrection of Jesus Christ.

John the Baptist is perhaps the most well-known messenger who prepared the way for Jesus. John preached a baptism of repentance. He told people they couldn't fix the mess they were in but that their Savior was on the way.

Though we now have the revelation of Jesus Christ, we do well to pay attention to the prophets and messengers of the Bible. Their voices can still call us to change, to turn away from evil and sin and toward grace and mercy.

There are also prophets and messengers among us today. Their work is not unlike that of the messengers who preceded Jesus. Today's messengers and prophets call us away from evil and toward good. They're just as unpopular today as they were thousands of years ago. No one likes to be told they're wrong, that there's a better way.

I hope we will listen to the prophets of the Bible, and I hope we will listen to the prophets of our own time. Prophets and messengers decry the evils of racism and sexism. They denounce the illusion that might makes right. They declare that money cannot create true value and worth.

We all need to repent, and the messengers are here to help us. This year, we aren't preparing for Jesus's first coming, but we are preparing for his second. And we are preparing to meet him in the last, the lost, and the least.

—*Scott Gunn*

Merciful God, who sent your messengers the prophets to preach repentance and prepare the way for our salvation: Give us grace to heed their warnings and forsake our sins, that we may greet with joy the coming of Jesus Christ our Redeemer; who lives and reigns with you and the Holy Spirit, one God, now and for ever. *Amen.*

—The Book of Common Prayer, p. 211

Splendor
Esplendor   Splendeur

On this outing, one of our first in more than a year, we ordered a feast: hand-squeezed orange juice, ham and goat cheese omelet, biscuits, and bacon gravy. Like most of the world, we hadn't eaten in a restaurant in a long time, and we decided to indulge.

Not until we set the menus aside did I understand that we weren't at a downtown diner but a heavenly banquet table. I had become accustomed to half faces, emotions conveyed with the squint of an eye or crinkle of the brow. Masks, wonderful gifts of protection though they are, hide the start of a smile, the contagious grin, the trembling of lips. Without the full face, it's hard to discern nonverbal cues.

Because the diners were eating and drinking, they weren't wearing masks. Since this was months into the vaccination period, I assume most were, like my husband and I, fully protected. The gift of that moment is hard to describe, the splendor of faces a glimpse into the divine.

At the booth nearest to us, two men held hands across the table. They laughed full-throated, throwing their heads back with abandon, their eyes sparkling. At another table, a young family sat, their toddler's smears of jam rivaling a Jackson Pollock. The beard of the man refused to grow uniformly, and a straggle of whisker caught a crumb of biscuit that the woman gently removed with her thumb.

At the diner bar, a man on the far side of middle age flipped through the weekend paper, his mouth a barometer of the headlines. He blew on his coffee and added more creamer, then returned to using toast to sop up runny eggs. Across the way, a table of three giggled like school girls even though they wore sensible shoes and shared pictures of grandchildren.

When Moses came down from Mount Sinai, the two tablets of the covenant clutched in his hands, the skin of his face was shining "because he had been talking with God." Exodus 34 tells us that Moses wore a veil on his face, but whenever he went before the Lord, he would take the veil off, "and when he came out…the Israelites would see the face of Moses, that the skin of his face was shining."

In one of the lectionary readings for the second Sunday of Advent, we hear these words from the first verses of Baruch 5:

"Take off the garment of your sorrow and affliction, O Jerusalem, and put on forever the beauty of the glory from God...for God will show your splendor everywhere under heaven."

On that morning, in a diner in downtown Cincinnati, God showed off in the splendor of these beautiful faces. No longer flat, pixelated images stuck in a square Zoom box, the faces were enlivened with the Spirit. I had forgotten how much God delights in each of us, how each of us is lovingly, carefully crafted in the image of God.

In a period of such sorrow and affliction, when the veils came down, the skin was shining, and between bites of egg and sips of OJ, I realized I was in the company of angels, basking in the splendor of God.

—*Richelle Thompson*

Fountain of life and source of all goodness, you made all things and fill them with your blessing; you created them to rejoice in the splendor of your radiance. Countless throngs of angels stand before you to serve you night and day; and, beholding the glory of your presence, we offer you unceasing praise. *Amen.*

—The Book of Common Prayer, p. 373

Repent
Arrepentirse   Se repentir

One of the most dramatic moments of the movie *Apollo 13* occurs after the spaceship loops around the dark side of the moon. A few hours earlier, a malfunction turned their vessel into a potential death trap. After observing the site where he was supposed to land and imagining the glorious lunar steps he'll never walk, commander Jim Lovell, played in the film by Tom Hanks, breaks the magic of the moment by looking at his crew and asking: "Gentlemen, what are your intentions? I'd like to go home."

The crew knows their purpose is no longer to land on the moon but to find their way back home. Their destination has changed. It is earth where they now place their hopes and dreams. And if they want to survive their accident, they will have to get to work—reset the computer, use the propulsion of the lunar module to escape the moon's gravity, and execute a procedure they have never practiced.

We often forget that the Greek verb that we translate as "to repent" basically means "to change one's mind or purpose." The editors of the renowned 1599 Geneva Bible already knew this. In the passage from Matthew 3:2 in which John the Baptist warns people to "repent, for the kingdom of heaven has come near," they added a marginal note: "The word [repent] in the Greek tongue signifieth a changing of our minds and heart[s] from evil to better." This is not to say that repentance doesn't include feelings of guilt and regret as well as penitential actions but rather that we should see those actions as part of a larger plan—perhaps like short legs of a lifelong roadmap.

As someone who spent years living in California and driving on its freeways, I do not like to think that all Christians, once we make the necessary correction on our spiritual roadmaps, will find ourselves driving on the same jammed freeway, making the same turns at the same spots and arriving at the same time to the same crowded destination.

In *Apollo 13*, collective endeavor is beautiful because it's not a lockstep march but an expression of teamwork. Once the course corrections are made, it still takes a village to bring the crew back home. Hundreds of NASA scientists help from the earth, and millions of people join in prayer for the astronauts' safe return. What if repentance also (or mostly) means helping each other along the way?

—*Hugo Olaiz*

Merciful God, who sent your messengers the prophets to preach repentance and prepare the way for our salvation: Give us grace to heed their warnings and forsake our sins, that we may greet with joy the coming of Jesus Christ our Redeemer; who lives and reigns with you and the Holy Spirit, one God, now and for ever. *Amen.*

—The Book of Common Prayer, p. 211

COMPASSION
COMPASIÓN   COMPASSION

Is compassion a visceral reaction or a learned discipline? I have been thinking about this question as I've studied the Book of Psalms. In the Psalter, certain parts and organs of the human body are often connected to specific emotions. The heart, for example, is the seat of love, thought, and memory. The wagging of the head expresses contempt. The gnashing of teeth denotes hatred.

Both the Hebrew and the Greek equivalents to the word "compassion" have to do with our internal organs. The Hebrew noun *racham* is a cognate with *rechem*, which means "womb." Compassion is thus related to motherly love and with the miraculous place where new life is created and nourished. Some Bible translations attempt to emphasize this connection by translating *racham* as "tender mercies."

The Greek verb *splagchnizomai*, "to be moved to compassion," is related to *splanchna*, a noun that refers to the entrails—

particularly the heart, lungs, liver, and kidneys. I first discovered this as a young college student when, reading the King James Bible, I was trying to make sense of biblical language about "the bowels of compassion" (1 John 3:17). Our lungs and heart respond instantly to our emotions—and didn't the father react as promptly when he realized his prodigal son was coming back to him? "While he was still far off, his father saw him and was filled with compassion; he ran and put his arms around him and kissed him" (Luke 15:20b).

When the film *Schindler's List* was released in 1993, the whole world learned about the life of Oskar Schindler, whose actions during World War II saved the lives of some 1,200 Jews. An ambitious businessman, Schindler didn't start hiring Jews to save them from the death camps. He first hired them because they were cheap labor for his factory.

Yet, at a certain point, his life priorities began to change. He eventually decided that saving his workers' lives was more important than making money. He argued to the Nazi leaders that the Jewish men, women, and children he had hired, including some with disabilities, were essential workers in Germany's war effort. Through pleading, scheming, and bribing, he managed to save their lives. In the process, he lost every penny he had made.

Oskar Schindler's story suggests to me that, in addition to being a knee-jerk reaction, compassion can also be learned—and improved by practice. Wouldn't compassion be a discipline worth cultivating?

—Hugo Olaiz

O Lord our God, accept the fervent prayers of your people; in the multitude of your mercies, look with compassion upon us and all who turn to you for help; for you are gracious, O lover of souls, and to you we give glory, Father, Son, and Holy Spirit, now and for ever. *Amen.*

—The Book of Common Prayer, p. 395

Readings for the Third Sunday of Advent

Canticle 9
Zephaniah 3:14-20
Philippians 4:4-7
Luke 3:7-18

EXPECTATION
ESPERANZA   ESPÉRANCE

He knew he was dying. I had been called home from across
the country. After a frail but intimate greeting in his hospital
room, my father looked straight at me and said, "Remember
what you promised, even if I don't make it another week."
He didn't. He died the next day, and his funeral was held the
Saturday after Thanksgiving, the day before Advent I. But
I kept my promise; we sang all seven verses of "O Come, O
Come, Emmanuel," his favorite hymn. My father's faith was
deep and private and full of expectation.

As Augustine of Hippo reminded us, "You have made us
for yourself, O Lord, and our heart is restless until it rests in
you." Our hearts are expecting to meet God. God has "placed
eternity in their hearts" (Ecclesiastes 3:11, CEB). We are
hardwired for expectation, and yet it can go so very wrong.
Holy expectation can easily be distorted by fear, competition,
privilege. Our expectations become demands or entitlements,
well-justified reasons why we deserve more than others or,
worse yet, are more worthy than our neighbor.

I love Advent. It is an entire liturgical season dedicated to (re)forming our expectations. From the first Sunday when we are invited to "cast away the works of darkness and put on the armor of light," we are being prepared to recognize what is to come. We are invited to repent of the ways in which our longings have turned us away from God and to "greet with joy the coming of Jesus Christ." At a mundane but not insignificant level, we are encouraged to practice restraint in a season of hyper-consumerism, focusing instead on practices of prayer, hospitality, and service. By the fourth Sunday, we cry out to God, "purify our conscience" because we know our worldly expectations are insufficient, often toxic. We need to be cleansed if we are to begin to understand the radical good news of the incarnation and the eschatological coming of Christ at the end of time.

I have no idea what my father actually believed theologically. What I know is that he expected to meet God at his death and insisted that we sing the song of his expectation. May Advent form and fill your expectations.

—*Lisa Kimball*

Come, thou long expected Jesus, born to set thy people free; from our fears and sins release us; joy of every longing heart.

—The Hymnal 1982, #66

SHARE
COMPARTIR   PARTAGER

[John the Baptist] said, "Whoever has two coats must share with anyone who has none; and whoever has food must do likewise."
                                                    —LUKE 3:11

It always cracks me up when people complain that the tithe as a biblical standard of giving is unrealistic. No one can give ten percent, they say. Well, if we spend a little more time reading the Bible, that ten percent seems like a real bargain.

John the Baptist says if someone asks you for your coat, you have to give them one, as long as you have two coats. That's fifty percent! And I think we can safely assume John means for people to be generous like that with everything they have.

Jesus makes it even more extreme. "So therefore, none of you can become my disciple if you do not give up all your possessions" (Luke 14:33). Got that? It's a one hundred percent commitment! So that ten percent starts to look pretty good, right?

Of course, the point of these instructions, whether the amount is ten, fifty, or one hundred percent, is that we should be quick to give away what we have where there is a need. After all, the scriptures teach us, all that we imagine we have actually belongs to God. We are simply caretakers for a time.

I will confess this is not something that I have perfected. On a good day, I practice generous giving. In our household, we give away money and things to those who have less than we do. We support the work of the church. I know how it feels to be generous, and it's a good feeling, frankly.

I also know what it feels like not to be generous. It's not uncommon, living in an urban core, to run across people in clear financial need. Sometimes I just keep walking. I know what it feels like to buy something we don't need instead of using that money to support those who don't have enough. It's not a good feeling.

God has been infinitely generous with us, offering us salvation not because of our merits but rather because of God's great love for us. God has created an unspeakably beautiful universe for us to inhabit. God gives us blessings beyond our ability to count them. Out of gratitude for all that God has done for us, we are meant to give freely to others.

I know from the times I get it right that this is what Jesus meant when we said that he came so that we "may have life, and have it abundantly" (John 10:10).

It's ironic, isn't it? To find abundance, we have to give away what we imagine we have. Jesus knew exactly what he was talking about when he said, "For those who want to save their life will lose it, and those who lose their life for my sake will find it" (Matthew 16:25).

When we share what we have, we may find that we have more than enough.

—Scott Gunn

O merciful Creator, your hand is open wide to satisfy the needs of every living creature: Make us always thankful for your loving providence; and grant that we, remembering the account that we must one day give, may be faithful stewards of your good gifts; through Jesus Christ our Lord, who with you and the Holy Spirit lives and reigns, one God, for ever and ever. *Amen.*

—The Book of Common Prayer, p. 259

EXULT
REGOCIJARSE   S'EXALTER

One hot summer morning when I was around seven years old, I remember sitting in my granddaddy's Baptist church in his hometown of Osceola, Arkansas. Granddaddy was a deacon in the church, so he sat by the altar. I sat on my mom's left, with my two brothers on either side of her so she could keep them settled. A woman sat at the other end of the pew, smiled at us, and proceeded to spread a towel across her lap. Perplexed, I turned to my mother to ask about the towel, and sensing my curiosity, she shook her head without turning toward me. I got her message: keep quiet; this is not the time for questions.

If you've heard our Presiding Bishop Michael Curry preach, the pastor sounded very much like that. Listening to the rhythm of the pastor's voice, I began to examine my surroundings. I noticed people leaping to their feet, shouting praises to God! In front of me, behind me, people jumped up with shouts of joy. Some were crying. The lady in the pew next to me had been wringing the towel as the pastor preached on. Then, she jumped up, waving the towel in the air and using it to wipe her sweat and tears. She jumped to the rhythm of the organist, who had started playing as the pastor's sermon reached a fevered pitch.

This experience was not entirely new to me, as all my grandparents were Baptist. My grannie's church in Somerset, Kentucky, shared many of these attributes of worship, but nothing compared to the exultation I witnessed in Osceola that day. When my sister in Christ got so passionate about her praise that she jumped up and shouted, she showed me what exult means in real life, not words in a text. She exulted God.

We use the word exult so infrequently; when I looked it up in the Oxford English Dictionary, the definition says it's obsolete. The prophet Zephaniah says otherwise: "Sing aloud, O daughter Zion; shout, O Israel! Rejoice and exult with all your heart, O daughter Jerusalem!" (3:14). In one translation of Luke 1:46-47, Mary says: "My soul exalts the Lord, and my spirit has exulted in God my Savior."

We're invited not just to praise God but to shout and sing loudly. At my church, our previous rector encouraged us to get loud with our responses at baptisms. He urged us to shout our responses to the baptismal covenant so people outside could hear us making our promises to God. How can we exult as much as we exalt? What might that look like for you as we await the birth of Jesus?

—*Miriam McKenney*

O Almighty God, you pour out on all who desire it the spirit of grace and of supplication: Deliver us, when we draw near to you, from coldness of heart and wanderings of mind, that with steadfast thoughts and kindled affections we may worship you in spirit and in truth; through Jesus Christ our Lord. *Amen.*

—The Book of Common Prayer, p. 833

STIR
AVIVAR   RÉVEILLER

As the AdventWord team met and explored possible words for this project, stir emerged as a favorite. The French language experts on the team shared fond recollections about their celebrations of Stir-up Sunday. This non-cradle Episcopalian had no idea what they were talking about.

Turns out, Stir-up Sunday is an old Anglican tradition. Across the Communion, some people still celebrate it on the last Sunday before Advent. In older prayer books, the collect for that Sunday begins, "Stir up, we beseech thee, the wills of thy faithful people." In the Episcopal Church, it's not until the prayer for the third Sunday of Advent that we hear the words, "Stir up your power, O Lord."

Over the centuries, Stir-up Sunday has taken on a very practical meaning: the time to "stir-up" the Christmas puddings. Traditions within traditions arose, with families (especially in England) gathering in the kitchen, preparing the tasty treats together. Each person takes a turn adding an ingredient, making a wish for the coming year, and stirring the mix. For those steeped in tradition, the stirring occurs east to west in honor of the journey of the three Wise Men.

While this tradition isn't as popular today, many homes still celebrate Stir-up Sunday. After the Christmas puddings are made, they are set aside to allow the spices, dried fruits, flour, and sometimes fortified wine to mature. They reemerge with great fanfare to be served on Christmas Day.

I love the idea of Stir-up Sunday as an allegory for our Christian walk. I have never made a Christmas pudding. But I've baked a gazillion Christmas cookies. I always look forward to those days. They end up being a long slog by the time we roll and scoop and dust and ice everyone's favorite cookies, but it's a day when we all gather together in one place, preparing for the coming feast.

We lick the spoons when no one is looking and peel warm chocolate chip cookies off the baking tray. We laugh and flick flour on one another and lose track of the number of eggs or tablespoons of butter. Every sense is engaged, swirling into a mix of past, present, and future, ensuring that the smell of cookies baking in the oven will always bring us back to our family kitchen, a place where we are connected by common cause and joined together in the work of stirring up.

—*Richelle Thompson*

Stir up your power, O Lord, and with great might come among us; and, because we are sorely hindered by our sins, let your bountiful grace and mercy speedily help and deliver us; through Jesus Christ our Lord, to whom, with you and the Holy Spirit, be honor and glory, now and for ever. *Amen.*

—The Book of Common Prayer, p. 212

GLADNESS
ALEGRÍA   JOIE

The Lord, your God, is in your midst, a warrior who gives victory;
he will rejoice over you with gladness, he will renew you in his love;
he will exult over you with loud singing as on a day of festival.
— ZEPHANIAH 3:17

In an earlier meditation, I wrote about our process of
selecting Advent words and how I happened to choose two
words from the same psalm. For this week, I managed to
choose two words that are in the same sentence of scripture!

Gladness drew me to it because it's not a word we say
much in our everyday language. But if you're familiar with
Episcopal liturgy, you hear the word gladness regularly in
the post-communion prayer. Sometimes when we hear a
word repeatedly, we can lose touch with its meaning. I found

myself curious, wondering what distinguishes gladness from a term we often say, like happiness?

Scripture gave me an answer to my wonders. I read Zephaniah 3:14-20 several times, but the word gladness would not reveal itself to me. Sitting in my car in the woods, frustrated at not connecting with this word, I closed my eyes and prayed. Perhaps one of the reasons I felt disconnected from the term was because I had not said the post-communion prayer for more than a year. Peace and justice are constant companions of my hopes and dreams for God's people. Gladness felt out of my reach.

Then I decided to read the entire book of Zephaniah out loud. If you can, I invite you to read this book to realize why it's part of our Advent lectionary. Reading books of the Bible in their entirety can't always happen in fifteen minutes, but Zephaniah prophesies in three short chapters. With my phone as my Bible, I began to read. By the time I got to the end, gladness had revealed itself to me. In the first chapter, after establishing his genealogy, Zephaniah prophesies about how God will reverse creation and bring devastation to Judah. Chapter two continues with more destruction because people fail to follow God and God's ways. But there is a remnant. And for those faithful people in Zion, God celebrates with a song of joy.

Journeying through this prophecy—from destruction, death, and devastation to joy and gladness—helped me fully comprehend gladness as a state of being versus a feeling or emotion. Jesus is the answer to this prophecy. The baby whose birth we await releases us from our sins and is God among us. God never abandons God's people. Instead, God rejoices with a state of being glad. God exults over us with loud songs of joy and reigns love over us. That's the promise God makes in God's Son, Jesus.

—*Miriam McKenney*

O God: Give me strength to live another day. Let me not turn coward before its difficulties or prove recreant to its duties. Let me not lose faith in other people. Keep me sweet and sound of heart, in spite of ingratitude, treachery, or meanness. Preserve me from minding little stings or giving them. Help me to keep my heart clean, and to live so honestly and fearlessly that no outward failure can dishearten me or take away the joy of conscious integrity. Open wide the eyes of my soul that I may see good in all things. Grant me this day some new vision of thy truth. Inspire me with the spirit of joy and gladness, and make me the cup of strength to suffering souls, in the name of the strong Deliverer, our only Lord and Savior, Jesus Christ. *Amen.*

—Phillips Brooks

Bountiful
Abundante   Bienfaisant

In the night when the crickets chirped and the house creaked, I cradled my growing stomach and worried. How could I possibly love this baby as much as I did our first child? My whole heart was hers, held in sticky toddler hands. Could I love our second child with equal passion, with the same abandon?

When the doctor placed our son in the crook of my arm, I knew in an instant my worries were for naught. I loved him with the same fervor as I did our daughter. Love didn't divide, with one piece of a heart here and another there. Like water, love sought out each crease and crevice, filling every space with a gracious bounty.

Fourteen years later, I cradled his face in mine. "Look at me," I urged, as his eyes sought solace over my shoulder, at the floor, the corner, anyplace except where he feared judgment and disappointment might live. "I love you without exception. I love you the same today as yesterday, and I will love you even more tomorrow. Being gay makes no difference in my love for you. It is without end. It is a love that is always." He fell into my arms, and I in his.

The window of human experience lets me glimpse the expanse of God's love. As a mother, I witness the depth of all-encompassing love of God the Creator. As a child, I bask in the immutable love of God the Redeemer. And as a wife, I feel the passion and succor of God the Sustainer.

The psalms try to capture in words God's love, but even in their perfect poetry and praise, they fall short. Paul's letter to the Corinthians describes love as patient and kind, rejoicing in all things and unending. Yet, even he acknowledges that we understand love now, "in a mirror, dimly," but only when we come "face to face," will we know God's love fully.

Perhaps the best we can hope for in our understanding is to believe without question Paul's words to the Romans: Nothing can separate us from God's love.

Nothing. God bestows the gift of love liberally, in abundance, bountifully. Our work is to live and love that truth in the world.

—Richelle Thompson

O Lord, you have taught us that without love whatever we do is worth nothing: Send your Holy Spirit and pour into our hearts your greatest gift, which is love, the true bond of peace and of all virtue, without which whoever lives is accounted dead before you. Grant this for the sake of your only Son Jesus Christ, who lives and reigns with you and the Holy Spirit, one God, now and for ever. *Amen.*

—The Book of Common Prayer, p. 216

SING
CANTAR   CHANTER

One of the most significant biblical references to song
appears in Exodus, when after crossing the Red Sea, the
people of Israel celebrate the Lord's triumph over the
Egyptians (Exodus 15:1-21). Many of the psalms encourage
us to sing to the Lord, play musical instruments, and
remember God's wonderful feats. The New Testament
elevates singing to the heavenly realm: angels celebrate the
glory of God (Luke 2:13-14), and the chosen sing in God's
presence (Revelation 14:3).

Yet there is also in the Bible another kind of singing—not
of celebration but lamentation. Some psalms express the
lamentation of a people who have been defeated, enslaved,
and forced into exile. "By the waters of Babylon we sat down
and wept, when we remembered you, O Zion," reads Psalm
137:1. I believe we could trace a genealogy forward from
Psalm 137 to the songs of the Civil Rights Movement and

even to the chants, "Hands up, don't shoot!" heard today at rallies protesting police brutality. This singing tradition has a double purpose, as it both names injustices and anticipates a day of justice. Presiding Bishop Michael Curry once said that antebellum slaves found hope and healing in the song, "There is a balm in Gilead," and poet Maya Angelou may have expressed a similar idea when she wrote that "the caged bird sings of freedom."

I grew up with parents who loved music and song, and perhaps that is why I have never been shy about singing in public. Three years ago, when media outlets began to show images of refugee children separated from their parents and caged on the southern border, I participated in a rally in my town. When they invited those present to share their thoughts, I went to the stage area and told the crowd what an honor it had been for my husband and me to meet Erik and Olivia, an immigrant family from Guatemala, and to become godfathers to their son David. I finished my remarks by inviting the crowd to join me in a song that I knew they would know:

> We shall overcome, we shall overcome,
> we shall overcome someday!
> Oh, deep in my heart, I do believe
> we shall overcome someday!

Let us sing to the Lord with horns, lyres, and drums. Let us praise God with guitars, keyboards, and even maracas. Let us sing songs of celebration and chants of denunciation and lament. Let us envision the day when all wrongs will be made right and we will sing with heavenly hosts, as written in Revelation 19:1b-2a: "Hallelujah! Salvation and glory and power to our God, for his judgments are true and just."

—*Hugo Olaiz*

Almighty God, who on the day when your Son was born gave to the shepherds a glimpse of your heavenly choir: Give us voices to sing songs of prayer and praise, lament and liberation, so that everyone may know your glory and enjoy your peace. *Amen.*

Readings for the Fourth Sunday of Advent

Canticle 15 (or 3) or Psalm 80:1-7
Micah 5:2-5a
Hebrews 10:5-10
Luke 1:39-45, (46-55)

* *This book is designed to be used during any Advent season. Depending upon the calendar, Christmas may fall any time during this fourth week of Advent. Feel free to skip ahead to the meditations for Christmas Eve and Christmas Day.*

BLESSED
BENDITA   BIENHEUREUSE

A friend of mine always responds to inquiries about herself with the response, "I'm blessed." Another friend, when we depart from one another, says, "stay blessed." Another friend of mine has a bumper sticker that reads: "Too blessed to be stressed." These friends are all Christian and African American, but the concept of being and feeling blessed crosses ethnicities and faiths. The state of being blessed takes on many meanings resulting from a combination of secular, Jewish, and Christian concepts. It's fitting that we use the word blessed to mean extremely happy, serene, and fortunate. Being blessed often results from someone who cares about us, loves us, or wants good things for us. I'm prone to refer to a good thing that happens to someone as a blessing. Being blessed involves love. The deeper the gift, the deeper the love.

When God blesses us, however it happens, we tend to want to tell someone close to us about it. Whenever something extraordinary happened to me, I knew I should tell my parents first, so I did. And yet, I had an elder friend named Joy whose counsel I often sought and whose opinion I cared about deeply. She knew me so well she could usually predict what I would say. Perhaps, like Elizabeth, the Spirit rested on her and informed her of the holy thing that happened to me.

Mary hurries to Elizabeth's house after the angel Gabriel visited her with the good news that she will bear God's son. Filled with the holy spirit, Elizabeth bears witness to the sacred in Mary. Elizabeth recognizes Mary as thrice blessed: blessed by God's favor, blessed with and by Jesus, and blessed in her belief in God's prophecy fulfilled by her. What I notice about this reading, now that I spent some time with the word blessed, is that the *Magnificat* is Mary's response to her cousin's exclamation three times that God consecrated Mary as sacred and holy. How much did Elizabeth's proclamation of Mary's blessed nature inform Mary's response? These thoughts reflect the power of reading and rereading scripture, listening to others read it, reading it on your own, reading it aloud—each time, God has something to tell us. For me, these recent readings revealed the importance of people who love us and contribute to and bear witness to our blessedness.

God loved the world so much that he sent to us his blessed son. God blessed Mary to bring Jesus to the world. As we wait for Jesus with an expectant spirit, add blessed to your thinking and your self-talk. Do you mean fortunate or sanctified? How does it change how you see yourself?

—*Miriam McKenney*

Blessed Lord, who caused all holy Scriptures to be written for our learning: Grant us so to hear them, read, mark, learn, and inwardly digest them, that we may embrace and ever hold fast the blessed hope of everlasting life, which you have given us in our Savior Jesus Christ; who lives and reigns with you and the Holy Spirit, one God, for ever and ever. *Amen.*

—The Book of Common Prayer, p. 236

FEED
APACENTAR   PAÎTRE

Feed my sheep.

We left the ham in the crockpot, stewing in pineapple and brown sugar and its own juices. The eggs were boiled and ready for deviling. The rolls lined up in formation, taking the time to rise while we were at church.

On Easter Sunday, we wore our best, and the ladies of the house sported corsages. The sun and skies and even the clouds conspired to offer a perfect spring day, crisp and bright and smelling of new life.

After the service, we didn't dawdle. Company was coming, and we had Easter to celebrate.

On our way out the door, we stopped. A man sat alone at a long folding table in the church's fellowship hall. His shoulders hunched. He wore a jacket over a sweatshirt over a t-shirt. His hands were dirty.

We introduced ourselves. Marvin was his name. He worked third-shift bagging groceries and came straight to church from the store. We asked about his plans for the day, and he shifted in his seat. A trip to the laundromat, he told us, without meeting our eyes.

Join us, we said. We asked. *We have plenty of food and room at the table. We'll stop at the motel and pick up your clothes. You can wash them at our house while we're eating.*

Come. Eat with us.

Feed my sheep.

The weather was brutal. The schools, which never cancel, canceled. The wind chill dipped below zero. Our eleven-year-old came down the stairs, bundled in layers.

A year earlier, I had added horseback riding as an extra activity at a summer YMCA camp. It was love at first sight, and our daughter was infatuated with all things equine. Her great-aunt fueled the fire, offering the proverbial gift horse in the form of a spunky pony named Princess. The stable and feed ran the equivalent of a monthly car payment but for a much different kind of horsepower, and the deal with our daughter was that she would have to contribute.

She got a job at the barn, scooping out manure, raking the straw, and bringing fresh hay and water to the horses. All for $1 a stall.

She was on the schedule for this afternoon. *Oh, honey, Daddy said he'd muck stalls for you today*, we told her. *It's too cold.*

She squared her shoulders, and blue eyes cast a glint of steel and determination. *It's my job*, she said. *I'm going. The horses are counting on me.*

Feed my sheep.

A man with a jar of water leads the group to a large room just outside the walls of the Old City. As they await the meal, they surely talk about the week, about the commotion at the temple, about the palm fronds on the way into the city. Sand and grime, not easily wiped away in the desert, cake their feet, and even with washed hands, their knuckles bear lines of dirt.

"While they were eating, Jesus took a loaf of bread, and after blessing it he broke it, gave it to the disciples, and said, 'Take, eat; this is my body'" (Matthew 26:26).

Feed my sheep.

—*Richelle Thompson*

Gracious God, the comfort of all who sorrow, the strength of all who suffer: Let the cry of those in misery and need come to you, that they may find your mercy present with them in all their afflictions; and give us, we pray, the strength to serve them for the sake of him who suffered for us, your Son Jesus Christ our Lord. *Amen.*

—The Book of Common Prayer, p. 279

GENERATIONS
GENERACIONES   GÉNÉRATIONS

What stories will you tell your grandchildren? When I was ten years old, Grandma Amelia took me to *La Gruta del Bosque* (the Grotto in the Forest), a labyrinth of sorts where children play hide-and-seek. Grandma sat on a bench while I played. Then she invited me to sit next to her and began to tell me family stories. She told me about the tiny rural village of her childhood. She also told me about *la luz mala* (will-o'-the-wisp). "Those night lights are produced by decaying animal carcasses," she explained to me, "but people thought they were an evil presence." Her stories were so vivid that I never forgot them. As a teenager, I began to collect family stories with a tape recorder—not only from Grandma Amelia but also from her brothers, sisters, and other relatives. I also started collecting old family photographs.

Generations is an important word in the Bible. It is a hopeful word, because it suggests that when we are gone, our children and grandchildren will still be around. In the first few verses of Psalm 78, the word appears four times. "We will recount to generations to come the praiseworthy deeds and the power of the LORD," the psalmist says, "and the wonderful works he has done" (Psalm 78:4). The main story that the psalmist wants the new generation to remember is that the Lord performs "wonderful works" and that we must walk in God's path.

In 1990, I moved to the United States for graduate school, but occasionally I would visit my family in Argentina. On one of those trips, I taped the interview that was missing from my wish list—the interview with my mother. "I have decided there is only one thing that will count when we get to the other side," she told me, "and that is how much we love people. All other accomplishments amount to nothing!"

I am very proud of the interviews and photographs that I have collected over so many years. Almost all the relatives I interviewed are now gone. When I play the interviews, I remember Isaiah 29:4b: "Your voice shall come from the ground like the voice of a ghost, and your speech shall whisper out of the dust."

Even though I will never have children or grandchildren of my own, I know that those stories and photographs will be preserved. I have nephews, nieces, and dozens of cousins who already have children and grandchildren of their own. I know that after I die, at least one of them will be as fascinated by those stories as I was when Grandma Amelia first told me about *la luz mala*.

What stories will you tell your grandchildren?

—Hugo Olaiz

O God of our people, before whose face the human generations pass away: We thank you that in you we are kept safe for ever, and that the broken fragments of our history are gathered up in the redeeming act of your dear Son, our Lord and Savior Jesus Christ, remembered in the holy sacrament of bread and wine. Help us to walk daily in the Communion of Saints, declaring our faith in the forgiveness of sins and the resurrection of the body. *Amen.*

—Adapted from a liturgy by the Anglican Church of Kenya

MAGNIFY
MAGNIFICAR   MAGNIFIER

And Mary said, "My soul magnifies the Lord, and my spirit
rejoices in God my Savior."

—LUKE 1:46-47

Mary has received the extraordinary news that she is to bear
the Son of God, and she has visited her cousin Elizabeth,
who has received her own astounding news that she will bear
John into the world. As you read the gospel accounts of these
events, you can almost hear Mary bursting with joy as she
proclaims what we now know as the *Magnificat*.

Mary rejoices, and she recounts the saving deeds God has
done in the past, knowing that God will continue to act
decisively in the world. But it's the first phrase that is so
arresting.

My soul magnifies the Lord.

How can the Lord of heaven and earth be magnified? Can that which is impossibly vast be made larger? Why does Mary magnify and not merely praise?

The Greek word that is translated into English as magnify is also translated as extoll, or honor, or exalt. But there is a clear sense in which the verb means that the subject is enlarging the object, hence the English word magnify.

Of course, Mary isn't really enlarging God, and the praise is perhaps coming from her whole being, not just her soul. When we peel away the layers of literal possibility, we're left to know this is exquisite poetry.

Mary proclaims with boundless joy and deep trust. She is bursting with faith and hope and gladness. God is enlarged for her, God's presence is looming larger in her life and in her future. Magnifies, indeed.

I've never experienced anything remotely like the reality-changing events of Mary's life. Still, there are a few times in my life when God's presence seemed more palpable to me. God didn't change; my perception of God changed in that moment.

There is a great deal we might seek to emulate in Mary's life. If God calls us to do something, we too will do well to copy her ready answer, "Here am I, the servant of the Lord; let it be with me according to your word" (Luke 1:38). We should hope we might possess a fraction of Mary's courage. But we might also pray that we could pour out a hymn of praise as Mary does in the *Magnificat*. It is poetic. It testifies to God's power in the present and in the past. And it assures those at the margins that God is on their side. All of this taken together magnifies God for Mary and for us.

Are you ready to magnify God?

—*Scott Gunn*

Pour your grace into our hearts, O Lord, that we who have known the incarnation of your Son Jesus Christ, announced by an angel to the Virgin Mary, may by his cross and passion be brought to the glory of his resurrection; who lives and reigns with you, in the unity of the Holy Spirit, one God, now and for ever. *Amen.*

—The Book of Common Prayer, p. 240

FLOCK
REDIL   TROUPEAU

"What's the first thing you think of when you hear the word flock?" I asked my daughters. "Chickens," said Jaiya. Kaia laughed and asked why she thought about chickens. Jaiya replied, "I was thinking of geese, but I said chickens."

We love to visit Spring Grove Cemetery and Arboretum in Cincinnati. Kaia and Jaiya go there together most days to walk, but because of dance-related injuries, Jaiya often stays in the car to draw, do homework, and read. She observes the Canada Geese who stop over on their journeys north or south, so they are frequent visitors of a particular area of the grounds. When their numbers are significant, we do our best to give them a wide berth. We know better than to walk near them because they're known to charge when they're in that big group. Even though we should have nothing to fear from a goose, there's strength in numbers.

Considering the flock in the Gospel of Luke, I think about the shepherds whose job it was to keep the flock together. They worked a third-shift job when most other people were asleep. They stayed awake to protect the sheep from predators. My friend, Jason Prati, reveals: "People saw shepherds as unclean. They lived with sheep, so they smelled. They raised sheep for Passover but were not allowed into the temple without going through purification. Shepherds heard this amazing news that they did not expect to hear, and they did not keep this news to themselves." They went to the manger, witnessed the birth, and told the town about it, or as Fr. Jason calls them, "God's flock." Those shepherds receiving the good news, witnessed by their flock, is a profound foreshadowing of Jesus's ministry to the poor, outcast, hungry, and sick.

As followers of Jesus, we've heard the connection made in the gospel of Luke between the flock of sheep whose shepherds hear the good news of Jesus's birth and Jesus as the shepherd of us, the community of God's beloved. This flock of the human family has strength in numbers, too. When we use that strength for good, a flock is a fellowship. When we collectively go in a different direction, away from love, the flock becomes a mob. It's hard to notice when one drifts away from the flock. But when we are a fellowship of a loving community, someone sees when one is missing. That's the Jesus who lives in us, driving us to keep the flock together in love. In a fellowship, every single person matters. When we are in a congregation, we see God in each other. How can we extend our flock to include all of God's beloved?

—Miriam McKenney

Almighty God, you sent your Son Jesus Christ to reconcile the world to yourself: We praise and bless you for those whom you have sent in the power of the Spirit to preach the Gospel to all nations. We thank you that in all parts of the earth a community of love has been gathered together by their prayers and labors, and that in every place your servants call upon your Name; for the kingdom and the power and the glory are yours for ever. *Amen.*

—The Book of Common Prayer, p. 838

Restore
Restaurar   Renaître

Restore us, O God of hosts; show the light of your countenance, and we shall be saved.

—Psalm 80:3

We might think of restoration as backward-looking. If a historic building is restored, the goal is to return it to the original appearance. Is that what the psalmist had in mind here? Is this a backward-looking psalm?

I don't think so. There's another way to look at restoration. When a painting is restored, the dirt and grime are taken away, and the colors shine forth as the artist envisioned them. Restoring a painting helps us see it as it was meant to be. The ancient artist's work almost comes to life.

Restoration can be about getting something to its original design. That is, I think, forward-looking.

I visited a workshop once where technicians and restorers were busy restoring old paintings. They had accumulated centuries of filth. As I recall, the restorers were attending to the material on which the artist painted. They were adding a bit of new paint or varnish here and there very sparingly. Mostly what they were doing was cleaning the paintings with incredible care.

When we pray for God to restore us, we are not trying to go back to some point in the past. Instead, we are asking God to restore us to the way we were made. To be restored, we're a bit like those paintings I saw in a conservation workshop. We need to have a thorough cleaning, to take away layer upon layer of sin. In some cases, we might need to adopt new habits or new ways of living.

Peeling away layers of grime on a painting isn't easy, and peeling away layers of sin in a person isn't easy. But just as a painting comes to life when it is beautifully restored, so too do people come alive when we discover the joy of living as God made us.

We are made to be hopeful, trusting, generous, merciful, and loving. Our culture often pushes us to be fearful, suspicious, miserly, vengeful, and hateful. Restoring us requires plenty of hard work, in which by God's grace we repent of selfish ways and turn to the Lord.

As this Advent season comes to a close, we do well to remember that Jesus welcomes everyone who comes to him, even at the eleventh hour. In our Christmas celebrations we are reminded that Jesus Christ came to dwell among us to show us what perfect love looks like. He restored human nature itself. We cannot be like Christ, but we can go on a restoring journey to become more Christlike one day, one decision at a time.

—Scott Gunn

O God, who wonderfully created, and yet more wonderfully restored, the dignity of human nature: Grant that we may share the divine life of him who humbled himself to share our humanity, your Son Jesus Christ; who lives and reigns with you, in the unity of the Holy Spirit, one God, for ever and ever. *Amen.*

—The Book of Common Prayer, p. 214

GREETING
SALUDO   SALUTATION

Of all the volunteering that I have done in church, none
have I enjoyed more than being a greeter. I love meeting
new people, but I also want visitors to have a truly positive
experience as they walk into the church. I want them to
see diversity. I want them to see that even folks who speak
English with a foreign accent (like me) are welcome.

Is it possible to be too enthusiastic when we meet someone
for the first time? Probably so. People argue about why Mary
was startled when the angel Gabriel came to her and said,
"Greetings, favored one! The Lord is with you" (Luke 1:28).
The salutation left Mary perplexed, pondering, "What sort of
greeting this might be" (v. 29). Was his salutation too loud? I
tend to think that she was perplexed because she thought she
was poor and she felt insignificant—not like a favored one!

The Latin version of Gabriel's salutation to Mary is *Ave Maria.* In the eleventh century, it became the first sentence of the prayer that we now call the Hail Mary. It was also the basis of the expression *Ave Maria Purísima!* ("Hail, Most Pure Mary!") that has been used as a greeting since the nineteenth century in some Spanish-speaking countries.

Although I restrain myself with those visiting my church for the first time, I tend to be quite effusive with people I already know. I shake hands with all the children. I hug women and some of the men. My friend Kathleen and I always exchange a kiss on the cheek. A rector once objected that I mentioned "kissing" in a report I wrote as a member of the Greeting Committee, and that objection deeply annoyed me. I grew up in a country where everyone, including men, kisses each other on the cheek! Didn't Paul end one of his letters asking church members to "greet one another with a holy kiss" (2 Corinthians 13:12)? I think we, as a church, are threatened not by holy kisses but by the perception that we are indifferent and self-absorbed.

Though I am respectful of boundaries, I will continue to be exuberant in my welcome. I want to surprise, even shock, people who think that my church is run by "the Frozen Chosen." Yes—I want those who visit my church to be as perplexed as the Virgin Mary.

—*Hugo Olaiz*

Dear God, whose Son Jesus Christ was greeted by a cheering crowd when he entered the city of Jerusalem: Send your Holy Spirit upon us so that we may greet each other with that perfect love that casts out all fear, foreshadowing the day when we will be greeted by your angels and ushered to our seats in the Paschal Feast, where you preside along with the Lamb and Dove, one God, for ever and ever. *Amen.*

Child
Niño   Enfant

So they went with haste and found Mary and Joseph, and the child lying in the manger.

—Luke 2:16

The birth of Jesus united earth and heaven in startling and beautiful ways. One can read the story, quite rightly, as a perfectly ordinary birth story, or at least as ordinary as the miracle of life can ever be. While Mary and Joseph have, shall we say, a complicated family situation, she gives birth with all the pain, beauty, and mess of any other birth. Joseph must have been a proud father.

One can also read the story as a singular event in human history, a manifestation of God's presence in a particular place. This birth is accompanied by signs and wonders. Angels proclaim God's glory. The heavens shine forth with a star to lead travelers from afar to visit young Jesus. This birth seems anything but ordinary.

Both stories are true, of course.

Jesus is fully human. He enters our world in the most vulnerable way possible, as a tiny child. Jesus is born in a remote backwater of the Roman Empire, a place that few people look toward as important. He comes into the world surrounded by family and ordinary people, not kings and courtiers.

Jesus is fully divine. He enters our world in fulfillment of ancient prophecies. Jesus is born as the culmination of dreams and miraculous births, the heir of David and promise of Israel. He comes into the world surrounded by angels and wondrous signs.

When we celebrate Christmas, we must hold both truths in tension. We cannot forget Jesus's humanity, nor can we forget his divinity. It is precisely the union of earth and heaven in this one person that changes everything.

We worship a God who is not remotely gazing upon us, uninterested in our hopes and fears. Instead, our God is willing to get right into the thick of it with us. Jesus Christ, Son of the Father, knows every human frailty and sorrow. And he knows every human joy and strength.

As we sing in the Christmas carol,

> Above thy deep and dreamless sleep the silent stars go by;
> yet in thy dark streets shineth the everlasting Light;
> the hopes and fears of all the years are met in thee tonight.

In Christ, our hopes and fears are met—not just at Christmas but every day for all eternity. That is worth celebrating. Happy Christmas!

—Scott Gunn

O God, you have caused this holy night to shine with the brightness of the true Light: Grant that we, who have known the mystery of that Light on earth, may also enjoy him perfectly in heaven; where with you and the Holy Spirit he lives and reigns, one God, in glory everlasting. *Amen.*

—The Book of Common Prayer, p. 212

About the authors

Michael B. Curry is the presiding bishop and primate of the Episcopal Church. He served parishes in North Carolina, Ohio, and Maryland and was the bishop of the Diocese of North Carolina prior to his election as presiding bishop in 2015. Throughout his ministry, Bishop Curry has been active in issues of social justice and reconciliation, speaking out on immigration policy and marriage equality. He has authored several books, including *Love is the Way: Holding on to Hope in Troubling Times* and *The Power of Love*, and is a sought-after preacher and teacher.

Scott Gunn is the executive director of Forward Movement, a ministry of the Episcopal Church that inspires disciples and empowers evangelists. An Episcopal priest, Scott travels widely as a speaker, retreat leader, and preacher. He is the author of the bestselling *Walk in Love: Episcopal Beliefs & Practices* and *The Way of Love: A Practical Guide to Following Jesus*. Before his work at Forward Movement, Scott was a parish priest in Rhode Island. He has worked in technology at nonprofits, a media company, and a university. He is also one of George T. Dog's humans.

Lisa Kimball is associate dean of lifelong learning and the James Maxwell Professor of Lifelong Christian Formation at Virginia Theological Seminary. She directs Baptized for Life, an initiative equiping congregations to nurture courageous Christian vocation in daily life.

Miriam Willard McKenney serves as Forward Movement's development director and is on the Way of Love working group. She was a children's librarian and school media specialist for twenty years before joining Forward Movement's staff. She finds extreme joy in parenting her three girls: Nia, Kaia, and Jaiya, with her husband, David. Miriam loves to evangelize about her love of outdoor fitness, even in extreme temperatures—as there is no bad weather, just incorrect clothing choices.

Hugo Olaiz works for Forward Movement as the associate editor for Latino/Hispanic resources and attends Holy Trinity Church in Oxford, Ohio. Hugo was born in Argentina. In college, he studied classics, linguistics, and translation. He lives in Oxford with his husband, John-Charles Duffy, and a terrier named Percy.

Richelle Thompson serves as managing editor at Forward Movement. A storyteller by trade, she worked as a journalist for several metropolitan newspapers before moving into nonprofit ministry, including a decade as the director of communications for the Diocese of Southern Ohio. She and her husband, Jeff Queen, have two teenage children, three dogs, a cat, and a horse, and call the bluegrass of Kentucky home.

About Forward Movement

Forward Movement inspires disciples and empowers evangelists. While we produce great resources like this book, Forward Movement is not a publishing company. We are a discipleship ministry. Publishing books, daily reflections, studies for small groups, and online resources are important ways we live out this ministry.

People around the world read daily devotions through *Forward Day by Day*, which is also available in Spanish (*Adelante Dia a Dia*) and Braille, online, as a podcast, and as an app for your smartphone. We actively seek partners across the church and look for ways to provide resources that inspire and challenge. A ministry of the Episcopal Church since 1935, Forward Movement is a nonprofit organization funded by sales of resources and gifts from generous donors.

To learn more about Forward Movement and our work, visit us at forwardmovement.org or venadelante.org. We are delighted to do this work and invite your prayers and support.